SKY HIGH
DUBLIN, WICKLOW AND MEATH

AN AERIAL JOURNEY

SKYWORKS

First published in Great Britain in 2009

British Library Cataloguing-in-Publication Data
A CIP record for this title is available from the British Library

ISBN 978 1 906887 43 8

PiXZ Books
Halsgrove House, Ryelands Industrial Estate,
Bagley Road, Wellington, Somerset TA21 9PZ
Tel: 01823 653777
Fax: 01823 216796
email: sales@halsgrove.com

An imprint of Halstar Ltd, part of the Halsgrove group of companies
Information on all Halsgrove titles is available at: www.halsgrove.com

Printed and bound by Grafiche Flaminia, Italy

Introduction

Dublin is one of the world's most gracious cities, with a history stretching back to at least 841 AD when the Vikings set up a raiding camp at the mouth of the River Liffey. Imposing squares, magnificent public buildings and elegant terraces survive as testament to its Georgian grandeur. Yet the city has become as cosmopolitan as any in Europe, a thriving business and commercial centre with a vibrant cultural and night life (as befits the capital of a country where half of the population is under 30). Now with a population of a million in the greater Dublin area, open spaces are greatly valued, especially Phoenix Park, one of the world's largest enclosed urban parks. Within striking distance of the city lie some glorious landscapes, country houses and historic sites. To the south in County Wicklow lie the Wicklow Mountains, rising up to 3927 feet at their highest point, and in their heart the ancient monastic site of Glendalough and the park and garden at Powerscourt. To the north west in County Meath, the Hill of Tara is one of the most symbolic and mystical sites in the whole of Ireland, while the town of Trim still bears witness through its medieval remains to its importance in the Middle Ages.

Seen from above, this spectacular mix of moorland and mountain and rich green pastures, mansions and monasteries and strong stone castles, and – in their midst – the bustling capital city, underlines why Ireland appeals so strongly to the heart as well as to the eye.

SKYWORKS

For aerial shots with impact, look no further…

Skyworks is an independent television production company and a stock footage library specialising in top-end High Definition filming from the air. The company has become one of the world's leading HD aerial archives for High Definition video and stills.

On the television side, Skyworks produces a range of factual programmes, varying from series about history, landscape and heritage to observational documentaries and more recently drama-documentary. Skyworks has produced over 100 factual programmes for international broadcasters, including the BBC, Discovery and ITV.

The Skyworks' team is systematically travelling the globe and filming locations in the unique style for which the company has become renowned. Skyworks' archive collection is already geographically broad and thematically diverse. The company's vision is to continue filming until the world has been covered and catalogued for all to see.

www.skyworks.co.uk

Merrion Square, one of Dublin's largest Georgian squares.

Merrion Square was laid out by John Ensor in about 1762.

The National Museum of Ireland–Archaeology, home
to some of the country's greatest treasures.

Trinity College, founded by Elizabeth I in 1592,
is Ireland's greatest seat of learning.

The view down the River Liffey
into the heart of the city.

A panorama of the south east of Dublin, out to Dublin Bay. Merrion Square is centre right.

Phoenix Park, to the west of the city, was opened to the public in 1745.

The Phoenix Column in Phoenix Park.

Phoenix Park covers 1762 acres and is the largest enclosed urban park in Western Europe.

Modern housing to the west of Dublin: most people live in the
suburbs of the city and commute to work.

Industry has tended to move out of Central Dublin to more
accessible sites on the periphery.

The landscape at Carton, a few miles to the west of Dublin,
once the seat of the Dukes of Leinster.

Carton was lost to the Leinster family after the seventh
Duke rashly sold his birthright to a moneylender.

Conolly's Folly at Castletown House, immediately to the west of Dublin.

Castletown House, built in 1722-29, was the first Palladian house in Ireland.

The Magazine Fort in Phoenix Park.

The River Liffey skirts the south of Phoenix Park as it flows into the heart of the city.

St Audoen's Church is the oldest medieval church in Dublin.

O'Connell Street is Dublin's main north-south highway.

The Custom House, designed by James Gandon
and built between 1781 and 1791.

The mouth of the River Liffey,
flowing out to Dublin Bay,
with Howth top left.

Dublin Airport, the country's busiest.

The view over Malahide towards the islet of Ireland's Eye and the Howth Peninsula.

Dun Laoghaire, a Dublin suburb and Ireland's busiest passenger ferry port.

The Port of Dublin.

The River Liffey rises in the Wicklow Mountains
and flows for 81 miles to the sea at Dublin Bay.

A plethora of yellow buses criss-cross the Dublin streets
– converging here at O'Connell Bridge over the Liffey.

Dublin Castle dates back
to the thirteenth century. It was
the centre of English rule in
Ireland and home to the English
Viceroys who represented
the British monarch until the
twentieth century.

The Papal Cross in Phoenix Park, where Pope John Paul II celebrated Mass in 1979.

The Hill of Tara, seat of the High Kings of Ireland until the eleventh century.

The rolling pastoral landscape of Meath.

Approaching Trim, a Norman stronghold on the River Boyne.

Trim Castle was founded in the twelfth century and is one of
the largest medieval castles surviving in Europe.

Ancient Ireland. Newgrange, a passage tomb built around 3200 BC.
The rays of the sun shine into the burial chamber at the winter solstice.

Modern Ireland. A dramatic motorway bridge, north of Drogheda.

Drogheda, a Norman port, formerly one of Ireland's most important towns.

Humewood Castle, County Wicklow, built as "an
occasional resort" for its owner in the late 1860s.

The setting of Humewood Castle in the rolling Wicklow landscape.

The Wicklow Mountains is the largest slab of continuous high ground in Ireland.

The underlying granite of the Wicklow Mountains is covered
in a blanket of peat which supports several heather species.

Glendalough is one of the most important religious sites in Ireland. Founded by
St Kevin in the sixth century, it continued as a monastery until the Dissolution in 1539.

Because of their proximity to Dublin, the Wicklow Mountains
have come under enormous visitor pressure.

The Wicklow Mountains were severely glaciated which has helped to
form their attractive mix of lakes, mountains and valleys.

Powerscourt House was begun in the 1730s. It was gutted by fire in 1974 but has been partially restored.

The gardens at Powerscourt are among the finest in Ireland.

Arklow, at the mouth of the Avoca River, has a great seafaring tradition.

One of Arklow's best-known sights is the Nineteen
Arches Bridge, the longest stone-arched bridge in Ireland.

The Great Sugar Loaf Mountain, looming over the holiday resort of Bray.